What people are saying  and his poetry

Jade's poems are powerful, vivid and, when you consider each one was written by a head rocking side to side, remarkable.

—Ron Corbett, *Ottawa Citizen*

Jade's story, told through personal letters and powerful poetry, is a moving lesson to all of us. Many young people will benefit from Jade's courageous sharing, but no matter what their age or circumstance, readers cannot fail to be uplifted by Jade's creative and brave spirit.

—Cathy Sosnowsky, author of
Holding On: Poems for Alex

Strength of the Human Spirit

JADE BELL

Library and Archives Canada Cataloguing in Publication

Bell, Jade, 1974–

Strength of the human spirit / Jade Bell. – Rev. ed.

Poems.

ISBN 978-1-894694-51-3

I. Title.

PS8603.E448S77 2007   jC811'.6   C2007-900997-2

Editor: David Stephens
Copy editor: Neall Calvert
Cover and text designer: Laura Kinder
Cover, title page, page 58, 65 photos: Mike Tannassee

First edition April 2006
Revised Edition February 2007

Printed in Canada

Granville Island Publishing
Suite 212 – 1656 Duranleau
Vancouver, BC, Canada V6H 3S4
Tel: (604) 688-0320 Toll Free: 1-877-688-0320

info@GranvilleIslandPublishing.com

www@GranvilleIslandPublishing.com

Dedication

I want to dedicate this book to the man who gave me hope when there was none to be found, who made me laugh when tears streamed down my face, who was there for me when I took my first and last steps, and who gave me the courage to carry on with life without him—

My dad, Tyler Bell

Acknowledgments

I wish to thank the following people for their help in bringing this book to completion:

- Neil Godin, for starting and going all the way through with my project, and for just being my friend.

- The Granville Island Publishing team, consisting of managing editor Jo Blackmore, designer Laura Kinder, editor David Stephens and copy editor Neall Calvert.

- Photographer Mike Tannassee, for the cover, title page, page 58 and page 65 images.

- Element and Associates Corporate and Project Finance Ltd.

- Last but not least, my two angels, Martina and Lindsay, for caring for me.

Thank you also to the Abilities Business Cooperative, an initiative of ConnecTra Society, which is affiliated with the Disability Foundation, and West Coast Group International for their generous contributions towards this project.

Table of Contents

List of Photographs

Foreword

Jade Bell's book is an extraordinary gathering of poems, songs, letters and photographs revealing deep love, excruciating struggle, and profound hope. The rhythms and rhymes, the words of the songs, attain sheer beauty:

> *Can you hear angels sing our story*
> *of pain as it tangles with glory.*

The book's title, *Strength of the Human Spirit*, accurately describes the cumulative effect of this collection – a renewed source of courage.

Ghosts are a recurring presence in this work and in the author's life. I am always heartened by reference to fundamental human spiritual experience.

Ultimately, this is a book to treasure, to admire. We respond to the voices given expression, as well as to the triumph of Jade Bell himself – over obstacles so tragic and daunting we can only be inspired.

—Bud Osborn, poet, activist
January 2007

Bud Osborn's book *Keys to Kingdoms* (Get to the Point Press) won the 1999 City of Vancouver Book Award. His most recent book is *Signs of the Times*, illustrated by Richard Tetrault and published by Anvil Press. Osborn, a director of the Vancouver / Richmond Health Board, was one of the first winners, in 2006, of the Kaiser Foundation's National Awards for Excellence in reducing the harm associated with substance abuse.

I know it's hard for you, Jade, to remember that your dad will never give up on you. I told you so many times that I would get you healed even if I had to pack you on my back to get you there.

     Love . . . Dad

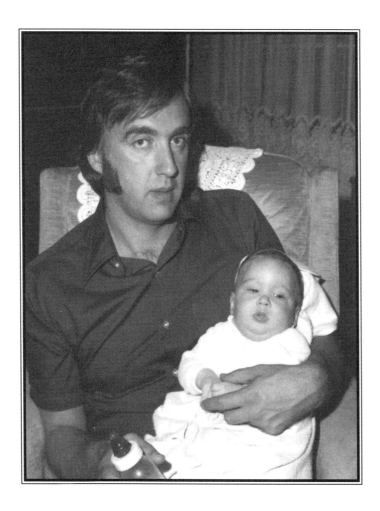

J ade, it's always a pleasure to read what you write. It makes my mind tumble back to a time when you first came to me as a little boy to practise writing stories. It was difficult at first for you, but as your confidence grew so did your skill at writing.

Sometimes when all is quiet I relive those memories, and they always leave me with such good feelings inside. I remember when you first started writing after your accident. It was a struggle for you to express the pent-up feelings that you held inside.

Today I read messages from a soul that is more at peace with himself. Your thoughts are well crafted and express your message well. There are some wonderful writers in this world. As the painter paints beautiful, breathtaking scenes on canvas, so too does the writer paint his beautiful pictures in the mind of the reader. As you start to read again, you will be amazed how you can learn to manipulate words to express your feelings. You have been writing poetry now for several years and this has helped to hone your skills. And you can go above and beyond your expectations with your level of writing skills.

Jade, you have the mark of a great writer. You have the two most important qualities: imagination and creativity. I can judge the difference between a good writer and an exceptional writer simply by reading the first half dozen sentences of a writer's work. Reading hundreds and hundreds of books has taught me to recognize the exceptional writer. And it's in you, if you want to develop it.

Remember the model of the hollow tree that we made and the model projects that you and Shay used to work on at my place – the soldiers and tanks? Those were great times.

Love you and Martina a ton . . . Dad

Father

My Father
He is my creator
When I was born he was there
   He is my teacher

From a little man he has been there
He is my mentor
His great wisdom and principles have always been there
   He is my knight in shining armour

With unconditional love he has been there
He is my saviour
For when I was going through Hell he was there
   He is my pillar

And if he should crumble
I want him to go in peace, and not to care
I would bleed out my eyes
   Yes I would cry

But with no lies
I promise, Father, I won't die
Because I'm a fighter
   And I'm a saviour

But part of you will live forever
Within the blood pumping through my veins,
   Right to my core

Your son,

Forever more

Christmas 2000

Those Who Never Cry Wolf

Let beautiful song birds
Sing this mime's broken words
   Down the winding roads
   Racing against clocks backwards
Disjointed within crushed time
Twisting and spiralling an outline
   How life can leave us behind
   Words of hope I wrote these lines

   Those who never cried wolf
   Who would only die for love
   Lord, please don't take my father
   For he is all I have

Cut it in half,
Blind to see a photograph
   Take the other half,
   My mind still hears us laugh
Echoing across the vast sea,
Summer past – the family tree
   Standing still within memory,
   Having the will not to let go of me

   Those who never cry wolf
   Who would only die for love
   Lord, please don't take my father
   For he is all I have

Streams flow under dreamy rain drops
Our dreams I see and aim as we walk
   Through lives that we embrace so precious
   In a wink of an eye for the two of us
Can you hear angels sing our story
Of pain as it tangles with glory

Without reasons or rhymes
We seal our fate in its time
So can you feel my tears within
Chase your spirit, saturating your skin
A man without fearing the end
Who will live forever in legends
Blue eyes that will help guide
Me through this darkness to the other side

So I made an oath
To never cry wolf
For the man who died for love
To keep strong
Till we meet again
And we all laugh
Running as children
Somewhere within oblivion
With all I have

Those who never cried wolf
Those who never cry wolf

February 26th, 2005

Could It Be You

The soul in a piano
Stirs and dances with each echo
    As the black and white ivory keys
    Sing out majestic melodies
Under an elephant's moon tear drops
Within a million memories that soon stop
    As black and white dice dance in this rain
    I take your hand to dance again and again
As white ashes bury our losses
I see the beauty in crushed magnolias
    That angelically float by us, in an hourglass
    As time just passes

    Could it be you
    Could it be you

An oasis of lost horizons
Feeling the warmth of the grainy sandpaper
Between your toes as you leave your footprints
Dancing in the wind
    Could it be you I see
    Lost inside those willow trees
Cloaked in darkness
Release your love and let
The sunlight through
Bathing in an ocean of beauty

    Could this be true
    Could it be you
    Could it be you

Icebergs submerge into cold waters
Gold veins spread out like God's fingers
Caught up in a breeze within a breeze
A million stories within this story
I take the blue prints for any hints
I dust off old photographs
    To attempt to bring you closer
    But your touch remains so distant
That blackened images fade through the light
    upon this page
To attempt to trace out your face
As you lifted my spirit somewhere safe

Could it be you
Could it be you
Could it be you

Please let it be you

I listen to the waves brush a shoreline
As we drift throughout the ages
    And I wait for some sign
    Lost within a mirror of time
Shattered words, missing pieces
Love burns a hole inside your soul
So I search in these shadows
    The scale shifts and twists
    The trail you left sinks or floats into an abyss
Is your name knotted within the skies
Or is it only an illusion that you said goodbye

Could it be you
Could it be you
Could it be you

Please don't let it be true

August 26th, 2005

So here we are in the darkest place. Not to forget you, I try picturing your face.

Blind to see pictures – but who needs pictures, Dad, when they only strip us from the now. I have too many good memories that I cherish about you – in mind, body and spirit – and will, so long as we are part of this earth or this earth is part of us. I think I can speak for everyone in this room, especially myself, who in your life and your passing you impacted with your intelligence, broad worldly knowledge and your old-soul's wisdom.

Some of us were strongly affected by your selfless giving without asking, your compassionate nature and kind, affectionate heart. Then there are a few of us, who had our lives completely changed because of your unconditional love and ability to forgive without judging a single one of us. I was blessed to have you for a dad, especially when I faced my biggest challenge waking up like this in September '97. I think you were the only person who was compassionate enough to understand my pain threshold, and it became part of your own. As you burdened yourself for nearly eight years with finding healers to free me from this self-incarceration, you never once complained about anything. You lived life so optimistically, and I began to live my life by following in your footsteps. I had a new purpose, goals, dreams and the perseverance to accomplish them.

Dad, do you remember being in Mexico, knowing your time with all of us was nearing the end? I will cherish every second of a lifelong second in memory of your example. One of your qualities shone throughout that entire journey. It was the ability, with these enduring words, to make your disabled son feel like the most important person in the world.

"We have some fantastic and exciting things to do ahead of us, Son, we really do, just you and Dad!"

You said the same thing over about ten times, so I would never worry about this day. After twelve years of worrying about when the next tragedy would happen, after we lost Aaron, and after having you by my side for all these years, I was beyond being worried about you. I understood my own brush with death, and this was the hardest five months for me to handle because I felt your psychological pain and loss.

As I sat by your side, not willing to accept the inevitable, we held hands and your calming voice said, "I'm lucky to have a son like you."

Then I said, "I'm luckier, to have a dad like you." And we shared our last tears together in that moment in time.

It had been a long twelve years for you and a long eight years for me suffering in our diminished quality of lives. As long as we kept our sense of humour, we shared so many laughs; it was our only means of just trying to keep our heads together. I will miss how proud I made you, Dad. I will miss having a dad to be proud of! You never once let me down. I will miss your unconditional love. I will miss us three guys! I forgot to ask you a question in the past. In this life of new beginnings, how do we write The End? I hope you don't mind me sharing a special brilliant thought you emailed to me in Ottawa.

> *To laugh often and much, to win the respect of intelligent people and the affection of children, to earn the appreciation of honest critics and endure the betrayal of false friends, to appreciate beauty, to find the best in others, to leave the world a better place than we found it – whether by a healthy child, a garden patch or a redeemed social condition – to know, even one life breathed easier because you lived . . . this is to have succeeded.*

Rest in peace, Dad. Your immortal beloved soul left with such grace.

You're A Distraction

You're a distraction
In the sand box of my imagination
    I sit with a box of new crayons
        Dictated by my puppeteers I burn by the stake
As a voice shouts out – *Paint a sand castle*

But time gets split by an atom
And I'm staring down at the canvas of time
Below the door in the floor
    Of an ocean of darkness
        Within a drowning clown's conscience
Drowning in your wake

Because you're a distraction
Your long black silhouette dances in the wind
    You're a bruise in my delirium
    You're my distraction

But time stops on a heart beat
An endless reflection
In this cyclone alone with me
I have become numb
    A lost equation of someone
As I look above the clouds
    And hand shake through the crowds
As we become cloud dancers
    Bathing in the sun with the music too loud
To hear our questions or answers
On just what this romance has become

Because you're a distraction
Your long black silhouette dances in the wind
    You're a bruise in my delirium
    You're my distraction

Boxed in, your glass tear drops
Shatter words in black
    Reflecting your curves that sang back
    Of this dark black magic beauty
That enchants my soul across the black sea
Bleeding from your eye of secrecy

As I feel your heart stop
As I lose your venom
    In the taste upon your blossomed lips

Suddenly you escape my finger tips
As you stain my veins
With red roses and black orchids

Because you're a distraction
Your long black silhouette dances in the wind
You're a bruise in my delirium
You're my distraction

And we dance under my skin again
My gorgeous mysterious poison
So gamble on what I see
On the black of these eyelids
And what once shone white, in the blackness
of the night

Is now gone within oblivion

August 27th, 2005

Blood in the Grass

A drop of blood falls in the park
   Leaves of golden yellows, tangerine oranges and
     deepening reds
   Weave within shadows, images, dreams on my eyelids
So misunderstood, a fool's autumn heart

So we're running down, falling for what we have
   In so deep
   I feel bliss within your distant heart beat
With a pocket of demons for you to love

Cut down by blades of grass
Chasing bloodless ghosts into the shade of our past
Chasing bloodless ghosts into the shade of our past
   As I hold my girl, in a world faded fast

   It's not love I'm running from
   It's numbers rolled on dice
   It's an unknown abyss
   It's the blood on the grass and what we've become

So dance with me, my love, within my heart beat
   Hold me suspended within your heart
   Hold me unclothed, close to you in the dark
And let our eternal dreams be sweet

Cut down by blades of grass
Chasing bloodless ghosts into the shade of our past
Chasing bloodless ghosts into the shade of our past
   As I hold my girl, in a world faded fast

September 1st, 2005

You're Like the Flip in the Coin

You're like the flip in the coin
   You dance like violence
   Under the sheets of silence
Sparkling silver top to bottom
Shattering beauty in pieces
   Taking any chances in this dance

Not knowing where you're going
   Head or tail, heads or tails
Over what face is up when it goes down
   Dead in a bed of nails
   I bleed the faces in detail
   That your beauty always veils

You're like the flip in the coin
   Sending my heart to soar
   Across the ocean of desire
Your beauty is so haunting
Feeding my burning flames
   In the ashes of this fire

Essence I ache for deep within bones
   But you're so distant
   Like a speeding bullet
The target remains to be unknown
   Give me some love and I'll feel it
   Give me some trust and I'll steal it

Because you are like the flip in the coin
   Someone carved your head
   Into a jack-o'-lantern
Twisting up a cyclone

That screamed murderous red
The tail trailed from the rings of Saturn
But I still held you close
    My lovely lonely spark
    That scars the stars in the dark
And shot a hole through my soul
    Hold me, my beauty, and eat my heart
    Then patch me up on the flip start

Because, baby, you are in the flip of the coin
Yes, you're in the twist of the coin
You're like the flip in the coin

September 6th, 2005

This Monster

A crumb falls to the ground
  As you just sit
Engulfed with sounds
As you crumble bullets
In the teeth of this monster
Into your eye of imagination
  A silent killer
Or just with a bubble gun
Are you scared yet
That you are a prisoner of war
Or that you're in the target
Of your silenced roar
  You stink of ink
And if you sink your teeth
Into this monster's trigger
  And just imagine
Before your very eyes ghostly figures
Carve out your imagination
In these establishments
  You chew cherries
Spitting out rolls of dice
With seeds that blow into the leaves
  You seem invisible
You look into a mirror
You see a full house of monsters entangle
And they all disappear
You tangle with restraints
That handcuff you to me
  As the monster paints
  Intangible beauty

In the reflection of your imagination
You dancing with me under sheets
Of rain and the monster appears as a gentleman
  Imagine this monster
  If you can
This monster that has conversations with mimes
  Through time and reason
  Through season and rhyme
  Chew on this
  It's your fabrication
Imagine the monster blowing you a kiss
  From his dark prison
His cage he sinks deep within
  Your bleeding unspoken, uneven pages
Un-wined the twine, break open the wine
  Let the wind scatter your thoughts into pieces
Then when you're back even, read me your favourite line
  About this monster with 10 toes, 10 fingers
  This monster

September 7th, 2005

Catastrophic Love – Part Two

I would walk to the end of this earth
Use my blood drops not to taint your curves
   Bloodier than love
A lover in the dark I can't forget
Bludgeoned red heart I use to paint your lips
   So look above
I once held you naked and heard you laugh
Burnt photographs and our love is all that's left
   That's what we have

   It's not the crunch that I'm scared of
   It's not being prepared to lose my love

If Hell froze, would screamin' faces freeze in ice
If heaven went up in flames, blackening the skies
   How would we know
If what we evolved instantly dissolved in a spark
Spirits soar eternally, raven ghosts into ebony we part
   Where do we go
I can see the sable sparkle in your eye
I see a cavity in the jet swarthy sky
   Out my glass splintered window

   It's not the crunch that I'm scared of
   It's not being prepared to lose my love

We will stretch out in an endless universe
Painting my love timelessly upon my weightless canvas
   Can you absorb it
Feel your black curls spiral, dancing vast and black
Through every star burning upon my ghost's back
   In the particle flaming abyss

In the unknown prophecies that swim in an ink bath
  As I walk to the end of this earth
  To paint your moonless orchids

  For your bloodless lips
  For your bloodless lips

Dead Man's Dance

The tastes aren't savoured
   In the salt in the sea
   In the ripples in water
   In the flavour of beauty

So who is this angel
   Who are those curves
   Who are those secret meetings
   Santa Claus bows with no applause

So take me to Mexico
   Take me to the very end
   Dammed to dance with this shadow
   As we twist in the wind

Bundles of bread to buy me time
   And where is my city
   Has everyone lost their minds
   But me, but me, but me

So who is this angel
   Who are those curves
   Who are those secret meetings
   Santa Claus bows with no applause

So what's next, my beauty queen
   Dodging bullets
   Becoming spies in these streets
We'll dance, my beauty
   In the shadows
   Of this dammed city

Who knows the spin in this maze
  Desperate minds scream
  Please pull me out of this haze
  And let my nightmares be sultry dreams

September 18th, 2005

J ade, I can understand your fears and frustration, and I realize how difficult it must be for both you and Martina at this time. I would also be concerned, as you are, with any further deterioration. But just be patient a short while longer. All that is lost can be regained and turned around with intensive physiotherapy, diet and vitamins.

I know what ridicule feels like, Jade, and it can be painful. But you must learn to use the pain to your advantage, as I have. I want my deals to succeed so badly I can taste them. The whole family thinks I'm an idiot. They can't understand why at 67 years of age I want to go to a steaming, disease-ridden country like the Philippines to chase after a pipe dream. How can I refute their opinions?

The truth is I can't, and furthermore don't have time to. I know what I have to do to succeed, and I won't quit. And neither will you, because you know what you need to survive spiritually.

So keep wanting it so badly that you can taste it. And you will win. You were not a failure in Ottawa. You proved to yourself that diet, exercise, no smoking and no alcohol do make a difference. That, in itself, is success. You learned discipline when you quit the use of alcohol and smoking. You were not a failure; you succeeded.

When people are skeptical of your ideas or goals, don't be upset. It's not their goal, so why would they care? If you want it so badly that you can taste it, you will succeed.

Be careful how you measure success. Even if you go to Brazil [to meet with spiritual healer John of God] and you don't stand up and walk home, it doesn't mean that you failed. No, you only fail when you quit. Somewhere, somehow you will be healed. And you're not going to quit trying. Because if you do, I'm going to pick you up and pack you to the door of success.

People who don't have health problems seldom believe in healers. Put them in your situation and they will look at it much differently.

God sent you a real gem when Martina came into your life. I admire her so much. I can't think of many young ladies that would be prepared to pack you up flights of stairs on their backs. Is Martina a pain in the ass sometimes? YES. But we all are, Jade. You are, I am, and everybody I know is. We can't be perfect all the time. So cut her some slack sometimes. She will go all the way with you to reach your goal of being healed.

All my love to two special people . . . Dad

Autumn Broken Dreams

When autumn doors fall open
Raking our dreams lying uneven
    And I lie on your pupils
And you're isolated in my focus
Dancing with you in silver bullets
In the wind we twist spirals
    Your hair shimmers golden skies
    Reflecting off the blackened eyes
Spirits tango, demons tangled my angel

> *But she smiles*
> *Over tangled miles*
> *Over broken dreams*
>   *And bent crocodiles*
>   *She just smiles*

We danced in the same dreams
Loving, laughing, living entities
Colours blend in that blackened pupil
    As we just get buried alive
Autumn shimmered beauty in love's eyes
Twirling to the end we twist spirals
    Sparkles of light in her tears
    Emotion of sight then you disappear
Spirits tango, demons tangled my angel

> *But she smiles*
> *Over tangled miles*
> *Over broken dreams*
>   *And bent crocodiles*
>   *She just smiles*

September 25th, 2005

Written In Stone

I walk in a play
Played out into flames
So we take hands and dance
As the curtain is drawn
Is truth a deception
I'll give you my credence
Just make your ink mark
And play out your part
Dance my blues to pieces

Sing my bitter sweet

A musical without the music
Phoenix fire wings they plucked
They finger-fucked my conscience
Angels of isolating pain
Demonic puppeteers write stains
Wet ashes burning these pages

Sing my bitter sweet
My facts in this play
My eclipsed obscure script
My words girl a world
Before it all melts away

If the burning bridges collapse
Spinning our compassed ghost maps
Wilted in the axis tilt
Demons and angels left behind
Through flaming rain we glide
Sparkled wet ashes they spilt
Sprinkled behind the applause

Played flames without their claws
Disjointed facts, acts, played out

Sing my bitter sweet
Sing with my script
Sing

October 5th, 2005

Jade, I'm very proud to see you using your tact, patience and good judgment. Now you are using your intelligence in a winning way. Always remember, "You catch more flies with honey than with vinegar." And the last part of your message is very beautiful to me. Thanks for the lyrics to those three songs. It would be great if I could hear the melodies. I'm sure that they are spinning around in your head. It would be a challenge to find a way to get them on paper.

Some of my books touch on what psychics can and cannot do. It has a great deal to do with your belief system, how flexible your mind is, and how far you are prepared to stretch it.

This is just a small installment of the information that I pack around in my slightly balding bean.

Love as always and forever . . . Dad

Sink

Would you sink in endless desire
Blood burns silhouettes in fire waters
　　In the vessel to my brain
　Holding me in an endless abyss
　Sinking in my melting waxed bliss
　　Scorching sparks in the rain

Would you sink into my hands
Would I sink into your flames
Would you sink into my passion
　Let love sink into our brains

Scorching heat that burns the insides
A twister, blistered wing that flies
　　Of joy and pain
　A slinky mystery sunken blue
　A creamy dream sinking within you
　　Burning my veins

Would you sink into my hands
Would I sink into your flames
Would you sink into my passion
　Let love sink into our brains

September 27th, 2005

As you know, Jade, I am a prolific reader. Many times I come across little gems that I so often would like to share with another soul who is intrigued by the power of the written word. So I've decided that, as we both like to express ourselves in writing, I should pass these gems on to you. Sometimes they will be but a few words – other times it could be a lengthy poem or short story.

Sing like no one is listening
Live like you've never been afraid
And dream like anything is possible

I love cooking with wine. Sometimes I even put it in the cooking.

Everyone has a photographic memory. Some just don't have film.

Going to church doesn't make you a Christian any more than standing in a garage makes you a car.

A balanced diet is a cookie in each hand.

Middle age is when broadness of the mind and narrowness of the waist change places.

Learn from the mistakes of others. You can't live long enough to make them all yourself.

Experience is a wonderful thing. It enables you to recognize a mistake when you make it again.

Each time a man stands up for an ideal or acts to improve the life of others or strikes out against injustice, he sends a tiny ripple of hope. And those ripples, crossing over each other from a million different centres of energy, build a current which can sweep down the mightiest walls of oppression and resistance.

God promised a safe landing, not a calm passage.

Love . . . Dad

Where Do They Go

On a street curb
Sits a super hero
   With tear blistered eyes
As the river of blood
   Echoes another car crash sunrise
Leaves on the trees burn
   Time stirs in shadowed nights
Where do heroes go when they die

Bent teeth pianos
In a corner he cries
   After dodging gold bullets
   Villains, mobs, gangs and spies
He looks over a dead man
   Time twists, shuffling a dance that glides

Where do heroes go when they die
Above the blue skies
   Below the whisper in the wind
   Into the sunset that lies
Where do heroes go when they die

Sitting on railway tracks
Drinking bloody wine
   In the middle of nowhere
We taste his bitter smile
Getting lost for miles
   Whispering a hero's tale
   We spiral through the ghost's eyes
Where do heroes go when they die

Tear drops fall from the sky
They sink into my skin
Wrestling demons that possess my insides
I unwind time deep within

   Under a hero that cries

   Under a hero that cries

Where do heroes go when they die
   Above the blue skies
Below the whisper in the wind
   Into the sunset that lies
Where do heroes go when they die

October 5th, 2005

Waiting

I sit in a vacant spot
Getting lost in a cosmic knot
        I feel it pulling my eyes closed
Buried with falling leaves
Dreamin' of my true love always
        Lying in snow angels upon this road
    Desolate silenced time I wait
    To blanket her within winter's cape
And off we heat the cold

Waiting for winter to fall

Dancing with the snow flakes
Gliding as we lie awake
    As our bodies melt the ice
Lying upon an eye of illusion
Painting the snow white canvas of a woman
    Lost under the falling skies

Waiting for winter to fall
    To feel her carved curves
    Finger painting with my starved nerves
Rolling down hills like snow balls

To come to a sudden stop
Lost within the ink that drops
    Upon these snow white pages
Twisting through the autumn breeze
    Dreamin' of my true love always
Shattered words, frozen pieces
Questioning reason within this season

Would she dance with a snow man
   Waiting for winter to fall
   Waiting for winter to fall

Sparkling snow crystal dust trails
Cascade a white wash over me, angel
   Let's just get lost
Into a shimmer glittering figure
I watch you dance away in the winter
   Frost outlines your ghost

Waiting for winter to fall
   To feel her carved curves
   Finger painting with my starved nerves
Waiting for her love to steal all
Waiting for winter to fall

October 15th, 2005

In Your Ice Blues

In your ice blues
   Do you hold the key
In this lying truth
   In the bloodiest seas

Or is that really you
Beautifully dancing this beast
Confused, bruised dancing shoes
   Dance these blues away
In the line of fools
   Dance these blues away

In your blues
   Do you see your hair unwind time
Shimmering golden moons
   Bloody red on white lines

Or is that really you
  Beautifully dancing this beast
Confused, bruised dancing shoes
Dance these blues away
  In the line of fools
Dance these blues away

In your blues
  Scalpel your finger prints
While whistling these tunes
  Broken heart paints the cement
Pitter patter the news
  With beautiful colours
Ebony jet shadowed hues
  Outline these monster's figures

  In your ice blues
  In your ice blues

October 19th, 2005

Here's My Ghost Beside Me

Where have all the reds gone
Smoldering scarlet
   Autumn leaves undone
    Where have all the greens gone
     The leaves melt
In plasticine puddled illusion
   Where did all the white go
    Is it cotton balls
   Falling upon hills of play dough

    What happened to me
    What can I see
    When I fall

   There's all that red blood
Trying to disappear
   In our bellies of mud
    There's all those yellow sparrows
Drawn with crayons
    Shattered glass rainbow
Where's all that black gone
   Reflecting in mirrors
On my eyelids of imagination

What happened to me
Is this all I can see
   As I slowly fall
Here's my ghost beside me
   She's my ebony prized beauty
   My hollowed eyes see all

    What happened to me
    What can I see
    When I fall

October 20th, 2005

Without Lines

I hear ghosts tap dancing
    On the door of my mind
Or rain drops falling
    On my floor as time slowly unwinds
The breeze holds leaves
Through timeless boundaries without lines

> *They start at the beginning of the end*
> *Timeless journeys we glide like stringless kites*
> *At the beginning of this wind*
> *Evolving dissolving entities we fly*

Crackling energies crawl from other sides
    Passing through anything in their path
Twisting bodies collide in time
    Feeling the curves of the earth
Twisting wire your sapphires braid twine
Trigger happy from birth to death

At the beginning of the end
    There's something I am searching for
At the beginning of the wind
    I sail in directions not known anymore

Whisky stains upon the ghosts' lips
    Give me a moment eternally not to think
Give me some answers that drip
    Your blackened innards to shed light upon my ink
Let life and death finally eclipse
So I can solve the evolved mystery within the
    missing link

They start at the beginning of the end
Timeless journeys we glide like stringless kites
At the beginning of this wind
Evolving dissolving entities we fly

Looking out the window of my house
This flesh bound soul's asylum of mine
Looking in the glass reflection at someone else
On my floor as time slowly unwinds
The breeze holds leaves
Through timeless boundaries without lines

At the beginning of the end
There's something I am searching for
At the beginning of the wind
I sail in directions not known anymore

November 2nd, 2005

The Child's Sacred Journey

Their inquisitive innocence
Their inner peacefulness
Their creative minds
The junctions of roads
The world to explore
Changes they behold in time

    The child's sacred journey

Mistakes and achievements
Glory and pain-born quests
Through the motion of life
Leaving their footprints
Upon this challenged planet
Kindred spirits born to unite

    The child's sacred journey

    The child's sacred journey

November 16th, 2005

Jade & Martina, I'm sorry I got carried away on another topic. The song is beautiful – all we need now is the right set of lyrics.

I will not be in Mexico for Xmas. After travelling as much as I have been in the last month and a half, I need to rest, Jade, or the bottom will fall out.

I have another reason for not being there, but it is far too deep and personal to explain. But because of who you are I know you will understand. There is a type of pain that I can no longer stand up to as I pack on the years. For me it's best to avoid it. But I don't want you to think that Susie [his longime companion] is responsible in any way about my not coming, because she is not. She would go anywhere I wanted to.

I love you both so much, and I hope that my not being there you will understand.

Love . . . Dad

She, Her Boy and Their Tree

Can you see the snow fall
   The boy making a snow angel
   His wide eyes full of fantasy
   Within this blanket of snow
Here with me upon the wall
Emotions of life, I write this story
   So close your eyes and try to focus
   Un-wrap your imagination, it's Christmas
      She, the boy and their tree
         Frozen to the core within my memory
      She, the boy and their tree

Can you see the snow crystals
   A dancing mist covering our trails
   Dawn opens our tree hunt journey
   It could have been metres or miles
She and I exist on this parallel
Smiles as delicate hands decorate its beauty
   So can you focus on the ghosts
   I un-deliberately chase into Christmas pasts
      She, the boy and their tree
         A blizzard of words to paint imagery
      She, the boy and their tree

Living in example of this wise man
Who dissolved like the snow in my hand
   He left me to stand beside my family
To be here with you, Mom, in the mountains
To feel your warm loving emotions
To feel the magic and beauty of our tree

So close your eyes and try to focus
Un-wrap your imagination, it's Christmas
She, the boy and their tree
The Christmas spirit doesn't exist under our tree
As she and her boy know, it's no mystery

The Christmas spirit lives and breathes within their tree

This is what I see, love the boy and see the love for she

November 16th, 2005

Black Winter Feathers

There is this shimmer
  Of black ink-bathed bodies
There are these tremors
  Of naked soft legs always
Clenched desires of winter's
Shuffling soaked dance of beauty
  Through the hot tremors
  Moist shimmering iced flaming leaves

Something escapes, a silenced scream
  Bonded by soiled ink feathers
Something awaits us in shadowed dreams

Tastes I have to savour
  Melting dripping black ice wings
Into flames we shiver
  It's brilliant to hear her sing
Clenched desires of winters
Hold me in your jaws, we're flying
  Forever would be too clever
  Devour without waste, time is ticking

Below ice, above flames, something in-between
  Bonded by pain and pleasure
Something shakes us in shadowed dreams

Dancing silhouettes in thunder
  Black birds spill inner words in an abyss
  Feeling inside your swarthy palace
As we lie as lovers
  Under a shower of shard pieces
Flaming shadows, jet feathers

I dip my dark ink within moistness

Are we merely mortals that dream we're crows
Or are we crows that dream we're mortal lovers
Something whispers the answer within shadows

December 30th, 2005

Inferno Desires

Desire, desire deep within
Desire liquidates our souls till there's nothin'
    Fire, fire molting ghosts in murmured sparks
    Fire that burns your name into my heart
Desire, desire soaks in passions
Desire saturates bodies on ashes till there's somethin'
    Fire, fire escape into my burning desire
    Bound by wire explosions of fire

    And do it again till we lie in our desecration
    In rain, sleet, snow or flames any position

Fire, fire disintegrate, torch our figures
Bathe me in honey fuel, light the match, take me higher
    Desire, desire is a razor of tremors over her
    Spark this art of passions, let it smolder
Fire, fire molting ghosts in murmured sparks
Fire that burns your name into my heart
    Desire, desire deep within
    Desire liquidates our souls till there's nothin'

    And do it again till we lie in our desecration
    In rain, sleet, snow or flames any position

January 11th, 2006

J ade, thanks for the long message. It's always good to read your thoughts. If what we refer to as our Karma had been programmed in another manner, things would, I'm sure, have turned out differently. There are so many books that I would like to share with you. It would be so interesting to listen to your thoughts after you had read them. Many of the books I've read involve the human spirit. I'm just finishing a 600-page book that was so interesting I had a hard time putting it down every time I started to read it.

There is so much that I can teach you about what I read and what I believe in – who and what we really are, what our reality is and how we have the right and the ability to completely control our own destiny. We have the power to self-heal. There is absolutely nothing that we cannot do. You would be astounded at the power that each person has at their command.

If you are interested, I will set up a special program for you and me to get together and discuss this whole subject. You can either have someone read one or more chapters of one of these books to you, and then we can meet to discuss the material, or I can read you a chapter and we can discuss it together. Or you might prefer to have several books read to you so that you have a base of knowledge that you can call upon. Doing it this way will allow your knowledge base to grow. Then, when we discuss any new or old books that we have read, we can have an intelligent, meaningful dialogue.

I want to learn how to control my mind so that I can influence what will happen in my five senses' world. And from what I have read this is possible. I believe it because it has actually happened to me, and I was aware of it. Although at the time I didn't understand what was happening.

No one else in our family really wants to understand what we, as humans, are really capable of, except you and me. And I'm so glad that I finally have someone who will understand when I talk about this subject.

When you see John of God you will be allowing him to convince yourself that you, and only you, are able to heal yourself. This same truth also applies to me. It may be hard for us to accept, but it is the truth. We have the power. We just have to find the key that will allow us to perform the miracle on ourselves.

I will see if I can condense the material in one of my books that covers the subject of sight. When you read this information you will be absolutely astounded.

Jade, if we can learn how to self-heal, that means that we can also heal others – either by doing it for them or by convincing them that they have all the power to do it from within.

I will wrap you in my spirit of love . . . Dad

Blue Eyed Raven

Dad, read me that one again
   Of conspiracy twisting
   Of lives falling like frames
As kings who cry and fools that sing
   Bludgeoned in torturing pain
Loving and laughing at sweet nothings
   Dad, please read these stains
It's blinding fishing for answers in this wind

Will we remember, or forget
   The beginning to the end as men
   Dad will you take my hand and dance me in
Strength of the human spirit
   Flaming frames fallen
To take flight as blue eyed ghost raven

Dad, keep reading, don't stop
   I'll write between the lines
   To bleed a black sea of thought
The answers in the breeze I'll find
   Drowning the mortal tear drops
As I just close my eyes
   Dad, please read this knot
It's blinding fishing for answers in this wind

We won't regret
   The beginning to the end as men
   Dad will you take my hand and dance me in
Strength of the human spirit
   Flaming frames fallen
To take flight as blue eyed ghost raven

Dad, read me this poem
   Of fortune and mistakes
   A creed of poisons for a lesson
With no open avenues for escapes
Will we dance at the end
   I hope you will wait
Dad, please share your wisdom
Till my skull becomes dust in its fate

Will answers saturate our secrets
   The beginning to the end as men
   Dad will you take my hand and dance me in
Strength of the human spirit
   Flaming frames fallen
To take flight as blue eyed ghost raven
As blue eyed ghost raven

February 15th, 2006

Suits of Humanity

There exist two doors
    As far as I know
Taking my hand inside this world
    Then having to let go
Of your spirit that soars
On a road unknown
And all that unfolds is words
    Entities imprisoned in the flow

Would you believe me
    If I told you
    How much I miss you
In this suit of humanity

Questions I forgot to ask
    Answers you can whisper
Do all saints have a past
Do all sinners have a future
    Are all men born innocent
Do all men die liars
    There's not a woman to trust
    In these broken heart murmurs

Would you believe me
    If I told you
    How much I miss you
In this suit of humanity

Can you send me a sign
    On this long journey
Of rising and falling tides
    Drowning in oceans of dreams

Hypnotized by the sapphire skies
   Would you believe me
   If I told you I never lied

Would you believe me
   If I told you I never cried
   Please believe in me
When I tell you I tried
   Taking my hand when I'm free
   Is it painless on the other side
Bonded to go through doors eternally

February 26th, 2006

J̲ade & Martina, all is OK with me and you. I understand your situation. I watched it from day one in the hospital. What you always have to remember is that I love you with all my heart. I can sit and close my eyes and instantly see my little *bean*. You and I were good buddies until Dad was no longer part of the family. After that, things got turned upside down. But the important thing is that they are upright again. We don't look back; we just look ahead and try to make our lives better and more rewarding. If you keep improving, you will make a great contribution to this family. I need strong, compassionate and intelligent children to guide my family when I'm gone. Never underestimate yourself; you have great contributions to make in the future.

All my love to my two most special people . . . Dad

Time To Say Goodbye

ROBERT TYLER BELL

July 22nd, 1937 – June 29th, 2005

I spent five months hearing my dad suffer the worst cancer he could have gotten – because for my dad, his brain meant his life.

He appreciated every aspect of his life, and considering the amount of pain he endured through the last twelve years, he never complained or sought any sympathy. He was a giving, gentle father who never asked his children for anything. So when he needed me to be there in Mexico for him, I felt privileged. A strong sense of honour overcame me to help him in his greatest fight yet – a five-month fight after the doctors had given him two weeks to live, a fight that ended last night at 10:30 pm in a room full of his family, friends and loved ones – all those who were strongly affected by his unconditional love in their lives.

His breath became shorter around 9 pm. At this time it became overwhelming for me, and I broke down in uncontrollable tears. Then around 10:15 pm Martina asked if I wanted to hold my dad's hand. I nodded yes. So I told him to come visit me in my dreams. Martina told him to help me heal, and I told him, "I love you, Dad."

He had his favourite album on, *Romanza*, in a small Bose stereo Susie bought him for Christmas, on the dresser by his head. I held onto his hand and said, "You can go, Dad."

Then I couldn't hear him breathing over the music. So I panicked and asked Martina, "Is he still breathing? I can't hear him."

She said, "Yes, but very shallow. I can see his chest, but he's going soon."

Then the last song was playing: *Time To Say Goodbye*, a duet with Andrea Bocelli and Sarah Brightman. Martina saw him suddenly open his eyes wide and look straight at me, so she yelled to Susie, "Come quick, Tyler opened his eyes."

Then three long breaths and his soul left his body and went to the light. His 100-pound body, that looked like it had been through the Holocaust, just sank in the bed at the end of its long journey, lifeless.

I was the luckiest man to have you as my dad. Wherever you might be now, I know it has to be better than this planet of never-ending pain and tragedy. As hard as it's going to be without you, I will never give up fighting to accomplish our dream. You fought with me for seven years. You left me with nothing but good memories that I will hold in my heart till its last beat, in this motion of life. Wait for me and I'll be joining you in the blink of an eye.

Jade

Commentaries by Author and Friend

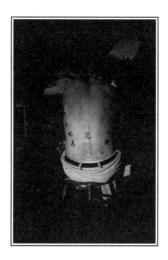

'Could It Be You'

Lord, I hope I'm wrong about this, but the song reads to me as though your father has recently passed; plus, there was that reference to your "mortal beloved" father in the email (a nice twist on Beethoven's "immortal beloved"). To me, the main theme of the song is the struggle to keep hold of someone when you can no longer grasp them in your hands. I think I'll leave my commentary short, in case I'm completely wrong about this.

Atrella

Your commentary on "Could It Be You" couldn't be more accurate. My dad was a very special father, and not a day passes that I don't think about the pain, suffering and tragedies we went through, yet still were able to laugh our tears away. I miss his company more than it is possible to imagine. I miss his dreams, hopes, affectionate heart, and yes, Atrella, I miss his touch. His hands were big bear paws that I held on his deathbed, as he once did for me at my bedside 8 years ago while I slept in a coma. He was a tough man who never complained about his own problems even as he suffered with colon cancer for 12 years before it caught up with him last February when it spread to his brain. The next 5 months will haunt me for as long as I am still a part of the living. Stories I'd rather leave out of this email.

Jade

'You're A Distraction'

It made me think of a love letter to an estranged wife; you know she's no good for you, but you desire her anyway, especially when the anniversary rolls around. The memories of romance, though, gradually give way to the memory of what she left behind when she left you for good. I hope that's okay, but I find it difficult to give you my opinion of something so personal. I just don't want to say anything stupid.

Atrella

I wrote this on the 8-year anniversary of my graze with death. The night I shut my eyes forever. That night I swerved out of control and crashed into the diva within heroin. It's a bitter moon anniversary for me with a lover who spilled my blood into ink upon this page. My self-destruction and creation.

Jade

'Blood in the Grass'

There's a certain desolation to "Blood in the Grass"; though it references autumn, it feels more like winter. I thought it had some great lines, especially "I feel bliss within your distant heart beat / With a pocket of demons for you to love" and "Chasing bloodless ghosts into the shade of our past."

Atrella

'You're Like the Flip in the Coin'

I have been over "You're Like the Flip in the Coin" more than a few times now; and although I find the poem quite moving with powerful and evocative imagery, I'm having a little trouble coming up with a theme that works consistently throughout. I have two theories, both of which are probably wrong, but I guess that's what poetry is for.

The weakest of the two is that the poem is an ode to a lover now departed, having either left or been pushed away. The theory I prefer is that the poem is an ode to your own imagination, which has created for you an entire universe to explore at will, a place free of all physical trappings and limitations; maybe that's where you go to find these wonderful words of yours. Of course, I'd love to know what it really means.

Atrella

'Catastrophic Love'

I was able to read "Catastrophic Love" a few times. It's truly beautiful, Jade. Well, as before, I'm not going to presume to know what these poems mean to you, but rather say what they mean to me. I read them as a meditation on the nature of death and the soul: whether we remain ourselves and retain our personalities after death, thus retaining that love we felt during life. If so, do we get to share our afterlives with our lovers, or are we alone, or are we with every other person who's ever lived? That last one sounds a bit like Hell to me. Or, worst-case scenario: what if there's nothing, your spark goes out, your soul (just energy) leaves your body, and you simply cease to be? That possibility is probably the only thing that scares me about death.

Atrella

'Where Do They Go'

I thought that perhaps this was about your father because of the high regard in which you hold him (hero) and what I thought was a reference to "Dead Man's Dance" ("He looks over a dead man / Time twists, shuffling a dance that glides"). Also, I don't think we've ever spoken of your brother, so it didn't occur to me previously; however, it does of course make perfect sense now. I'm guessing the line "Echoes another car crash sunrise" is a reference to how he passed?

Atrella

'Here's My Ghost Beside Me'

For some reason, I first thought this was about falling into a state of lucid dreaming, probably a response to some of the imagery ("hills of play dough", "yellow sparrows / Drawn with crayons"); but now I think it's about dying, and not because of the word "ghost" in the title. The autumnal imagery alone points to this, as fall represents nature's decline into its own form of death: winter. Then, there seems to be a reference to returning to the earth in the lines "Trying to disappear / In our bellies of mud". Finally, I can't think of any other state in which all colors, even black, are stripped away, but all is revealed nonetheless.

Atrella

It has nothing to do with death; it's the world as I see it. Looking through my blind eyes with my imagination I use artsy imagery to give the reader an idea of how twisted my blind window of perception is. The "ghost who sits at my side" refers to the way I "see" living entities: they are nothing more, or less, than black shadows in my world.

Jade

'Without Lines'

Well, if one were a fervent believer in the existence of the afterlife, then one would view the 80 or so years spent on this planet as merely the beginning; moreover, death would not represent an ending, but rather "the beginning of the end," which is something the author almost seems to be looking forward to, or at the very least does not fear. Death marks the start of a whole new adventure with destinations unknown. It also holds the promise of knowledge not to be learned on this plane of existence, though I find it unfortunate that one must probably die before learning the meaning of life. I like the contradiction in the lines "Give me a moment eternally not to think / Give me some answers . . ." Finally, death represents freedom from the prisons we create for ourselves, whether real or imagined, an eternal life without boundaries, unregulated by matter or time.

Atrella

Found Letter from Dad

Hi, Jade & Martina:

I just opened up your message and read it in its entirety. I will comment more on it later.

Two experiences that I must share with you before I go to the other side. I see you and me walking together down a tree-lined path. I have my arm over your shoulder. Jade, I've seen that vision a thousand times. That's what I mean when I say that I think of you every night when I lay my head on the pillow. And my next vision is you being introduced on the stage of The Courage to Come Back ceremonies a second time. I will give a brief introduction of why we have returned and then you will speak to 2000+ people about how you fought your way back from despair, darkness, and Hell. And that you are there to stand as an example of courage and determination for all those people who so desperately need to believe that if you want it bad enough it can happen.

You have changed since those very dark days of 1997. I can see it in the way you express yourself in your writing. This is the mature version of the little man that used to come to Dad's house to learn how to write stories. You can be a great writer if you are willing to work at it. And when your eyesight returns you will have a chance to expand your mind by reading the thoughts of some very special people.

Remember, Dad is with you every night. Loads of love for my two special people.

Love . . . Dad

About the Author

In his teens, Jade Bell was a handsome, popular, 6' 3" athlete, an A-student, musician, poet and potential film-maker. Unfortunately, Jade also had a dark side. He actively indulged in alcohol and drugs.

One night in 1997 when he had just turned 23, Jade went to a friend's house where, intoxicated with alcohol, he mixed a concoction of cocaine and heroin and shot it into his arm. He collapsed and was rushed to the hospital, where he lay in a coma for two months. When he awoke he was absolutely normal at first, but then he once again slipped into unconsciousness. The next time Jade woke up, his entire body was damaged by acute muscle disorder. He could no longer speak – worse still, he was also blind.

In this new, dark and desperate world, the unconditional love and inspiration of his father, Tyler Bell, taught him the true strength of the human spirit. One day something just clicked, and Jade decided he had something valuable to share with kids who face the temptation of using drugs – something that few other people still living could offer.

With help from his dedicated caregivers, Jade began touring schools in Vancouver and Alberta and, more recently, in Western Quebec. He speaks to high school students – more than 100,000 over the past few years – about the horrors of drug use and the effects of an overdose. He shows a video clip, *The Wrath of the Dragon*, that reveals the seamy side of the Vancouver youth drug scene and talks about the wasted life waiting for those who consider or continue doing drugs. Then he plays a brief speech he created that took him two months to write. (Jade can't use his hands or body. But by moving his head from side to side, and touching sensors on each side, he is able to tap out messages using Morse code. A computer records the coded taps and translates them into words. Without this technology, he would be silenced.)

Jade says that before this tragic experience he had an "invincible, nothing-can-hurt-me" attitude as a teen. Today, many a hardened or troubled youth with that same bad attitude has broken down in tears at the sight of Jade's uncontrollable body, beautiful blue, unseeing eyes and the power of his story. Though it's strange to think of his plight as a "gift," it's one that Jade bears courageously and gracefully with a knowing smile.

In 2002 he was presented with the Coast Foundation's Courage To Come Back Award in the chemical dependency category.

Jade lives independently in Vancouver, BC. In between his school tours, Jade spends his time responding to the flood of emails from students and teachers that inevitably follow his visits. He composes poetry and song lyrics to support his campaign. His website, <www.jadebell.ca>, features poems, a photograph gallery and current tour news.

Jade Bell is truly one of Canada's contemporary heroes.

—written by David Newing